A Legacy of Honesty

by Chaz Hudson, The Dislexic Poet.

To June.

Hope You Enjoy!

The Dislexic Poet :)

Front Cover Designed by Chaz Hudson, Bethany Bedell and
Stacey Green

Front Cover Artwork and Lettering by Bobby Penafiel and
Luke Melia

Illustrations Inside by Chaz Hudson

MISSTAKES INKLUDED.

This Book is Dedicated to All My Life Savers:

The Accountant

The poem that started all this was a poem i wrote for you it was an apologie and a thankyou all in one, this poetic journey started with sadness and pain and contined to were we are now. We have a stronger friendship phone calls are now about poetry, performing and travelling. youve helped keep me alive, visited from miles away just to see me for a weekend and supported me. There maybe miles between us but some how your always here.

The Sidekick

Well whats a superhero without a sidekick your my best friend and your family, youve heard my poems more times than i dare to count, answered thousands of phone calls to answer questions to help me edit my work, we worked on the cover of this at 3am and have had conversations about it been published loads well its finally happened, thankyou for always sharing in my excitement and been by my side on this journey! love ya buddy!

The Pants

Well what can i say about you i could fill this dam book with what we've been through together the up's and the down's. This book, The Dislexic Poet and me wpuld definitley not be here if it wasnt for you, your friendship and the hell youve been through to keep me here ill be forever thankfull, youve given me ideas how to get my poetry out into the world and no matter when i need your help in poetical matters you always answer your phone, there would have been many missed buses and trains therefore missed performances without you· Thanks Pants i hope i make you proud·

The Getaway Driver

The miles and miles you and your poor car have taken me is crazy you drove me up to edinburough for the ediborough fringe festival all that way for a day trip we didnt get home until 3am but you did it because you want me to jump at every opportunity· thankyou for practicing and trying to keep me calm before i perform· youve heard nothing but a legacy of honesty from me while ive been getting this ready for piblsihing and youve continued to be so supportive so thankyou· I hope theres many more poetic adventures to come·

The Monkey Butt

You are one special dude your the reason i questioned and wrote two versions of behind closed doors the one who told me i should be performing, filming and posting videos on youtube and facebook you saw talent in me that i could not see· thankyou for always being such a supportive young man! i hope that i am someone you can look up too (well look down too you know what i mean Mr 6ft 2)

The Grey Haired Supporters

Well without you i wouln't have cat sitters, id not be able to travel as far to poetry events for as long or as far as i have done, youve donated to my fund raising to help me achive my goals, answered many many phone calls from me to tell you what exciting things ive been up too thankyou for all the support you give im so lucky to have you!

The Poet Yoda

If it werent for us being put in touch with each other, all of this wouldnt have happened even in my craziest dreams (A dyslexic doing poetry ha) but here we are, your so dam pushy and wont take no for an answer thankyou for that. With your help ive gone from cowering infront of an audience and looking at my feet, to learning how to project my voice and when and where i need to pause or read slower ect, you also taught me how to use a mic (yes there is a wrong way) Youve cntinued to support me in any way you can so thankyou The Dislexic Poet would not be what i am today without The Poet Yoda

The Belivers

Well you two saw something in me that i couldnt see through the fog of mental ill health you saw strenght and belived that i'd find my way eventually, with your help ive stayed around long enough to find it doing somthing i love and really enjoy thankyou.

The Archer

"I am Awesome" the first words i ever said to you and for some reason you genuiley belived it, youve visited me at my worst, youve left me sometimes not knowing if youd ever see me again, ive hated you, refused to speak to you and thanked you, youve helped me through some tough times and listened on the phone to the good times· youve helped me understand myself better, your a rare one in your field thankyou!

The Girl with the Suitcase

I've not known you very long but we got really close really quick we've helped each other through some tough situations, youve even helped save my life a few times too· Youve always seen my poetry as something to be shared with people, thankyou for your support and the chances to perform along side you and be apart of your shows its always a privalage but most of all im thankful for your friendship Miss Skinner·

The Warrior

We met in a community centre in leeds you were in a rush but you still wanted to take the time to introduce your self give me your contact details and tell me you liked my performance and loved what i stood for since then weve never looked back youve given me some amazing oppurtunities which has taken me to london to perform and has given me a chance to work with vunerable people· ive never felt less around you which is amazing thankyou for your support and encouragement.

The Backers

I could list names that would fill this page you all know who you are, the Canadian poet who first inspired me and helped me to write down my thoughts and feelings, your the furry lemon who always keeps my imagination ticking, youve donated, youve suppoeted me in my mental ill health battles, practiced with, you are all the doctors and nurses who put me back together in the northenr general hospital, The pysiotherapist who got my body to the best it could be, staff who saw past my mental ill health in kendry and saw me underneath, the hostel staff who always saw potential in me, the housing officer who is still supporting me today, The friends i made in uni you guys were awesome, the first kid who came up to me and told me he was inpired by me stay strong and thanks Josh the memory still makes me smile, the Police officers that have on countless times saved my life and always had compassion and empathy for me, The Canadian Comedian who always supports my endevours, everyone who has shared there life experiances with me, all three of my support workers in university, the people who sent parcels and letters to me in kendry to make me smile, The 2D guy who's always a message away, De Montfort university staff who are still encouraging me, the staff at blakeway who worked on the voices in my head documentry and always made me feel strong, powerful and have continued to cheer me on since filming ended, the girls who were excited to recieve a signed socks poem which still makes me smile, the old cafe lux crew who has seen me at my worse (in hospital pj's) and my best, to anyone who has ever let me perform, the neighbor who checks on me and helps if im struggling, and anyone else taht has ever asked if im ok and needed to talk.

You all have one thing in common you all made me feel stronger, no longer ashamed of the words mental ill health anb suicide.

Because of all of you

The Dislexic Poet is stil here

I am still here

I survived

This is my legacy,

A Legacy Of Honesty

Meredith, With Love

Thankyou.

You are a flashlight,

When im curled up in the dark afraid and alone,

You are the bringer of light.

I fear i'll need you more than you'll ever need me but know if you do ever need me then i'll be the mirror of what you were for me.

See you're not always here for me but somehow your always there for me.

Like gravity pulling my body back down to earth,

You pull my mind out of the dark clouds and bring my thoughts back into living.

Like gravity i can't always see you but i can always feel you here.

You are faith...

Faith is me believing the words when you say that i'll never be too broken for you, you'll never run so fast that all i see is dust, things will never be too hard for you..

Cause HOLY SHIT! times have been hard.

For all the phone calls you answer just to hear me in a depressed state crying and saying how much i needed to leave you behind.

For all the times you answer the phone at 2am when no one else is awake just to listen to me having a break down and repeating the words i don't know what's happening to me, i don't understand, i don't know what's happening to me, i don't understand.

For having the patients to listen and talk to me to try help me understand.

See when i'm scared and at the end i can hear you singing james taylors you've got a friend,

Suddenly i can breath!

Suddenly i can take a step back!

See we've been through quite alot together you and i.

You've been there when i've been at my worst and very ill.

I remember you where there when i woke in the hospital just so i had something good to wake up too.

I remember you felt so much sadness and pain, at the hands of me and my actions.

Everyday I'm sorry that my mental illness hurts and causes you pain.

This is me in some way making a start to say how much you mean to me.

That my life would just not be the same without you in it.

Because with you here...

With you in it···

I'm starting to heal.

I'm starting to understand…

Alright people, follow me...

...let's go.

Chapter 1

Who Is The Dislexic Poet?

Hi there my name is Chaz otherwise known as The Dislexic Poet and yes you've guessed it i have dyslexia.

Why i hear you ask did i decide to name my poetic self after one of well what i thought was a weakness really for that exact reason i always thought dyslexia was a barrier to the written or spoken word, i still struggle to understand other poets metaphors in there poems i also feel not good enough because of my dyslexia in the poetic community this is one of the main reasons i choose The Dislexic Poet (no it wasnt spelt wrong on purpose i didnt know for two months until my friends informed me) it gives me a mask a braver version of me a poetic superhero if you will i can gain confidence to perform and share everything ive been through with total honesty which can help and inspire others.

The Nep Is Mighter Than The Sworrd

I am a Dislexic Poetic Superhero

I have to read by example

My cape is a black t-shirt

That reads The Dislexic Poet

So my invisable disability is visable

I wear it on my chest to inspire

I wear it on my chest as a badge of honor

I thought dyslexia was going to stop me achiving

But because i've overcome

Issues with my self assteme

I've not only been able to share im dyslexic

But i've turned the key

Opened up and shared

What's been locked inside of me

All the emotions and thoughts

All the struggles through situations

My dislexia and my poetry

Have helped me to connect

They've both helped to save me

If i could go back and see the younger me

I'd say keep your head held high kid

Just look who you could be

Back then i didn't know i was dyslexic

I only saw what people saw in me

Which happened to be stupidity

Now though

Things are very different

My Dislexia

Has been lauched from

Dis to Ability

It's helped make me the poet and person

I am today

Now i'm a Dislexic Poetic Superhero

To show others the posibilities

And to ask them what they see when they look
at me?

I am a Dislexic Poetic Superhero!

My Secret Superpower

Poetry could be a three line Hiku

It could be written by people in pain

Poems could be shakespears sonets

They can be written by soliders that will never quite be the same

I want to share what poetry means to me

Poetry is freedom of expression and speech

It let's me start conversations that need to be said

I've got hearts and minds to open people to teach

Poetry is the best therapy for me

I write when i'm upset and sad

When things get too much and i start to struggle

When i don't understand why i'm feeling so mad

Poetry is my written fire escape

My raw emotions tend to ease

As the words are written

It seems I've caught a poetic disease

Poetry can give anyone a voice

Writting makes me feel less invisable

When i hear people having conersations and connecting

It makes me feel like my life finally has value

Finding poetry makes me feel like i've found my superpower

I've found something that i love to do

Although i still have to practice speaking to crowds

That i still find really daunting it's still all very new

I write to make you feel uncomfortable

To tell stories that are unspoken and untold

I write to put you in someone else's shoes

So that you can hear everyday hero's stories unfold

I don't no what poems and poetry mean to you

But i hope i've changed your perception

Because this is what poetry means to me

It's only writen by dead old guys is a common misconception.

Dislexia is not the enemy

When i was young i struggled to understand

Comma's in grammer and i couldn't spell

I struggled to read and remember

I loved the idea of english but the adverage classroom was hell

I found out in university it wasn't because i was dumb

For years and years i thought i was defective

My brain just learns a very unique way

I was born quite dislexic

I'm a kinaesethic learner i learn by doing

When i read the words don't always stand still

I get the letter's D's B's and P's mixed up

To do english with dislexia definitey takes strong will

I absolutley love to write poetry

It's something i seem to be good at

I just have to have a little more patience

Keep trying and that is that

People told me what i couldn't do all the time

A small amount of people focused on what i could

As a kid i felt small and stupid

Who'd have thought i'd be here in adulthood

I maybe dislexic

I maybe a little slower

People just have to be patient with me

Coloured overlays ease the strain

Stops the words i write from running away

Dislexia has hit my confidence to read

Sadly overlays can't keep my nerves at bay

I like to read even though i struggle

I can only read young adults books

Big font books i find easiest to read

Even those books i still read quite slow

The most difficult thing i've found

Is dislexia interfere's with my mail

I struggle to read letters and understand bills

I'm an adult but this makes me feel like i fail

There's one dislexic secret i still haven't shared

I get embarrassed when i say i still can't tell the time

I know it's not my fault it's like trying to read chinese

I shouldn't even care cause what the hell i can write poetry and rhyme.

DYSLEXIC

Chapter 2

My Mental Helath Timeline

Trigger Warning

So you've learnt about my struugles with the written language now if you stick around youll be getting to know me a hell of alot more these next poems are about my serious struggles with mental ill health

Ive Struggled with mental ill health since 2013 ive had impatient admissions and sadly many trips to the emergancy department of the hospital. In 2015 while in hospital recovering from a suicide attempt from a 60ft railway bridge i discovered a poet who inspired me to start writting to get my own feelimgs and emotions off my shoulders i was feelign alot of guilt about how much id put my family and friends through so my first poem came from that. The following poems have been written over the years since, but a performance that i was to be apart of helped me to discover that i had actually written an acciddentla timeline of my battles with mental ill health, the struggle with surviors guilt, suicidal thoughts and my struggle to stay in the light they are brutely honest so buckle in it's going to be a bumpy ride.

Fun Fact It was actually in one of those impatient admissions that i came up with the title A Legacy Of Honesty i was worried about how impulsive my menatl health can be and i wanted to have soemthing to leave behind something that would explain what i had gone through it would also be a chance to tell people what they ment to me and thank them for all there support.

It's Just The Two Of Us

*this is what I hear the voice say

It's just the two of us

This stupid voice and i

Sometimes it gets me so down

All i do is break down and cry

*Your useless no one wants you around!

It's just the two of us

When i'm admitted to mental hospitals

Trapped with people i don't know or trust

Trying to act well, give the doctors right signals

*Your so shit shut up no one wants to hear you!

It's just the two of us

When the doctors are asking how i cope

It was just us two as i leaped from the bridge

Yet i was so alone when my bones were all broke

*Your a failure go do it right! JUMP OFF that bridge again!

It's just the two of us

Even when i feel empty and alone

Your always there shouting and yelling

When talking to Samaritens on the phone

*Why are you wasting there time no one cares.

It's just the two of us

Because you helped my friends all leave

I was always so down and depressed

I honestly thought they'd stay i feel so naive

*Why would anyone want to be your friend.

It's just the two of us

When i'm laid in bed for days

When i'm trying to ignore the suggestions you make

Seeing suicide in a 100 different ways

*What a joke you've failed so many times dickhead.

It's just the two of us

It has been so god dam long

Sometimes i get so scared

Will i still be me when your gone?!

Marianette

Can you see them? No?

I think

I'm the only one that can

I've tried to cut them

Again and again and again

It doesn't work

See there still there

I get tangled in them

They are attached everywhere

They remould my smile

When i want to go one way

They turn me the complete opposite

Sometimes i walk around in circles

I don't think thay know

That i know

But i do

I can finally see them

You can't but i can

Somedays i would love

For them to move

Move my legs, hands something anything

But they don't

Then im stuck in my bed,

Stuck in my bed with all my thoughts stuck in my head

I try to cut them with pills

But the pills aren't sharp enough

Somedays i get a false sence

Of control of freedom

Freedom of movement

But pain reminds me

That there still attached

It gets to me

Just as a ticking clock in a silent room would

I try to cut through them

Over and over and over and over

But they remain

It's as though i'm trying to stop the sun from rising

See? look?

There still there can you see them?

An Open Letter To Death

You are my childhood home

A memory i cannot forget

The thought of you is a warm blanket and the bed when i'm depressed

When i'm down it's a bed i bon't want to get out of!

You are an escape from the endless pain and suffering in my own head, the pain i need so desperatley to end!

You are a ghost of an old friend waiting to greet me once more

You are the thought i'm most afraid of on days i'm doing ok when i'm actually managing to tredd water

On the days where i'm drowning in a sea of sadness you are my best friend holding the life vest

We can't choose the fact were given life but we can all choose when to end it

You are the happy ending to my sad story

When your fighting endless battles day and night someone's got to win the fight?

Right??

It's sad when a promise of no tomorrow is more needed more desired than the promise of another sunrise

When people say there's so much left to live for the colours of spring, the beauty of a setting sun they don't realise it's been years since i've seen the world in colour!

Sadness sadness Sadness Sadness sadness Sadness
sadness Sadness
sadness sadness
Sadness Sadness
sadness sadness

Keep Of The Tracks

These days

My whole world

Revolves around

Keeping off the tracks

But at the same time

Keeping on the right track

See i bounced back from oblivion

But

This battle between David and Goliaf continues

Me been David but with pebbles not a rock

See when my day crumbles around me

My thoughts go straight back

To

Escape

To

Walking back onto the tracks

To

Leaving this god dam three dimentional plane

To you

This might sound insane

Come try on my trainers

I'm a size 7

See through my view finders

I have a distorted world view

I'm been brainwashed and recondtioned

To think everything i do is never good enough

See to the outside world

This skin of mine looks tough

Inside me my thoughts are crappy trapese artists

Balancing on an extra fine type rope line

I'm trying to see and believe the truth

And sift through all the lies

That are constantly whispered in my ears

There are odd days i can dare

To bare enjoyment

Where

Keep off the tracks is merely a sign

On days

Where a creepy guy in a black robe

Lerks in my shadows

Keep of the tracks

Is a sign of support

A sign something out there wants me to breathe

Stuck fast

Simply means unable to move

Thank God

Because if the sign where able to move

Then maybe i would have moved

While the train was still moving

It stayed stuck fast

So i stayed stuck fast

The trained past.

Are These My Last Thoughts?

Crumpled socks in my trainers

Speeding heart in my chest

The feeling of last

The last time

My hands touch these weeds growing through the cracks

They feel both soft and rough at the same

The wind is cold against my nose

The chill runs down my neck

As i feel the hairs raise up on my arms

My jeans are tacky sticking to my legs because of the rain

My trainers keep slipping off the ledge where there perched

Freezing mental under my bum is making me shiver and making the metal parts of me painful

I feel every bit of the scars from last time

But hopefully this will be the last time

The last time my tears will meet the rain as they run down my face

I feel lost

I feel alone

I feel afraid

I feel this maybe the last time anyone sees me.

End Scene and Encore

I'm staring at the great beyond

I'm struggling today

Just as i struggled yesterday

I'd love to look forward to future days

But the voice always drags me back

I'm shuffling on this narrow ledge

Less then a foot wide

Time has created cracks

Time has made crumble of this stone

A person standing here at 3am

Is less than safe

The mental river below

Glisens with the tears of my ancestors and the moonlight

Such a peaceful scene

On any other night

I'm staring into what may come next

As a voice shouts my name

I turned

A blue Flashing light and sirens filled the street

He was stood there all in black

With a flourescent torso

I turned away

As though turning away from

My own ticking clock

My own fleshy blanket

Away from everything and anything living

My mind was filled with

cloudy, misty, fogness

But my legs could still function

Unprompted one last time

Less than an ich

Between me, this ledge and the open air

Nothing but the bitter winter wind surround my body

As rode the escalator down

No life flashed before my eyes

No regret filled this body

Just darkness

See my thoughts

Were like cloudy lemonade

Unable to see, want or need

Anything but this moment

The gravel harshley cushioned my body

The grass knealed before me like i was a GOD

My stargazers

Where souless for a while

No life was wanted here

Next a scream

That caused earthquakes

Burst ear drums

Echoed in souls and

Yet created small smiles

It began with blue Flashes surrounding a street

It ended with blue flashes reflecting off the metal river

With the Sirens echoing a distant tunnel.

Lucky Escape

Laid in this hospital bed

I've just woken up

From the attempt on my life

You talked me into

I should have realised you were only pretending

You were never a friend

You told me you cared

That you understood me

That no one else wanted me around

I believed you

You took my isolation and used it for you own gain

You wore me down

Day by Day

Word by Word

With each day i was a step closer

To almost losing this fight.

Laid in this hosptal bed

With broken limbs

Broken bones

Arms and legs unable to function

Having all my independance taken away

You helped push me off the edge

You and your words of poison

You've taken so much away from me

A fully functioning left hand

My friends

My happiness

The ability to walk without pain

My life will never be the same

Because of you and your words!

Laid in this hospital bed

What doesn't kill you makes you stronger

Maybe not physically

Cause i'm actually quite broken

But mentally i'm like

Steven freaking Hawkin

Mentally···

I'm going to beat you into submission

I'm going to be a supernova

In the darkness you've caught me in

See i survived

I had a lucky escape

You should have tried harder

Cause i'm still alive and your going to suffer

Now your the one who should be afraid

Trembling in your boots

See i stared at death twice

It rejected me!

Your all out of cards my friend

I, i have a full deck!

Breathe

Everyday I feel Guilty

That i'm still here

And your gone

I suppose thats wrong

Cause it's not my fault

You took your last breath

And i'm still here

They laid you to rest

And yet i'm still here

Trying to be

The best me i can

But i still feel guilty

That i'm here

And your not

See

You raised thousands for charity

You were a great mum

The best officer on the force

A dad who took his kids to football games

You were a fire fighter

Strong and brave

And i'm just me

Who tried to take my own life away

I couldn't stand the thought of another day

Where you'd have given anything for one more day

But i still get to be here

And your still gone

I struggle with this guilt it tears me up inside

There are still days

I don't want

To take another breath

On those days the guilt almost eats me alive

You were a gran who took care of everyone

Around her

A child of five with terminal cancer

Who's loved ones

Would've trade anything for an extra day

So why am i still here

Nothing i can do can take away this guilt

That there's air in these lungs

That i'm still here

and your

Just gone.

Lay Down Your Mask

So i know that you now know

That i hear a voice that

You can't hear

But did you know Just how much

That voice makes me fear

Everytime i meet a new person

I get scared

Laid alone at night i cry

More than just one tear

Because i opened the door of friendship

And you willingly stepped right in

What will you do if i lose my battle

And i'm no longer here

All the time your hearing this

Your thinking Chaz

Just think of all the positives

Don't be getting hooked on all the negatives

Buts it's because i care

For the people around me

See i surround myself with all the good ones

The world has to offer

In my poetry i lay my soul bare

I drop all my armor

So this poem i had to write

Because writing helps me to cope

And at this moment this is

What's keeping me awake at night

See you see bubbly and cheerful

Funny and happy

You hear my sad stories and messages

In my poetry

But no one sees

When i almost stepped in front of a train

One night on my way home from leeds

My head was filled with so many bad thoughts

My body was filled with so much pain

Now i know sharing this with you

Some of you won't look at me again the same

But you know that's o·k

Because i know that i might also

Have helped destroy someones shame

Or at least made a dint in it

See i want you to know

And i want you to see

That i don't play pretend

If i'm honest with you

Then i'll be more honest with me

Because been fake won't help me

And it definitly won't help you

So i admit when i'm down

When i feel like i'm drowning

And i just can't cope

Because then people share with me

Turns out there's alot of other

People in the exact same boat

I just need to open my eyes

And take a look around

At everyone else trying

To get back

Up off the ground.

Phoenix

I want people to see me for more than my biggest mistakes and failures

More than just the pain and hurt i've caused

That my light will shine brighter than the darkness i'm fighting

I want to be what my friends believe i can be

Achieve more than i think i can

I've looked into the face of my friends and seen in their eyes that they worry i Won't be in thier futures

I can't promise what tomorrow holds but just maybe

My trembling hands will put down the gun, the knife

That my body will no longer be balancing on the edge

One day i'll survive my last battle and one day i will win and end my own war!

I will slay my own demons just like buffy

I will stand at the top of the mountain i'm climbing step by step everyday

One day

See strength isn't always visable

People are always telling me i must have something strong inside me to keep fighting

To Keep facing my demons everyday

They say they can see my light sometimes

Through the cracks i make in the darkness that tries to consume me

See i would like one day for darkness only to exsist when i turn out the light or blow out the candle

One day maybe i'll get to tell my children about the battles i've fought and lost and the wars i've fought and won!

I believe that tomorrow will come and things will get better!

Aslong as your alive to witness it!

See i've hit the bottom, had my body literally scarped up off the floor

I've risen from my own ashes

Just like a phoenix

And i am still here

I am still here!

Get The Ballifs In

You!!

You my friend you happen to think you know me

Call me a stuttering retard

A f**king Idiot

A pathetic mess

You put me in pain

Cause my body to hurt so much

That i can barely move

But you are nothing!

I am so much much more than

The weak insults you throw at me

They will not stick

I will no let them

You don't no my limits

See my strength

It stretches as far as the eyes can see

I can move moutains

With the strength god gave me

I could make the earth quake

I could cause tidel waves

With the strength i hold inside

Don't underestimate me

See you!!

You will not define who i am

I am not your puppet

I am a force to be reckoned with

In spite of you!!!

I will not just survive

But I will live!!

Chapter 3

The Darker Side Of Life

Trigger Warning

Glad your still here with me because these next
set of poems were written to shine some light on
the issues that i am very passionate about soem
of the poems where written for pacific charyties
or companies that also are very passionate about
subjects that arent spoken about often enough.

Behind Closed Doors!

He clenches his fists it's happening again

One more smashed bottle the kids run to hide

They have a routine now it happens that often

They put there hands over there faces and watch
as there mother is terrified

This small dark space they hope is safe

In the closet holding each other shaking scared

He's been in their lives five years now

Calls himself their step dad it's clear he doesn't
care

This woman so kind hearted and caring

He's hitting a woman less than half his size

Trying to protect herself hands up

She begs him "Please Stop" with teary eyes

She's bleeding from her ears still it goes on

Now laid still on the cold kitchen floor

The girl covers her little brothers eyes

She knows her mum can't take anymore

The girls had enough hugs her brother Tells him
stay in the closet hidden and safe

Her young heart pounds in her chest

She suppress the fear puts on her bravest face

She walks straight into the lions den

With as much strength as she can conger

One giant blow to the head

She manages to knock over the giant monster

The step dad now enraged

Stands back up puts the girl in her place

He's shouting and yelling

Blood now drips from this young girls face

The girls gone quiet not one more scream

He kicks her and hits her till she can feel no more
pain

Her poor mum unconscious and bleeding doesn't
no things will never be the same

Her brother lets out an ear piercing scream!!

The man looks down see's what he's done

His heart starts to race

Panic takes over he slams the door and begins to run

The little boy sat on a bloody floor sobbing

The neighbours heard the screams they no somethings not right

Nobody knows the sight that awaits

The blue flashing lights were a little too late but awfully bright.

Behind Closed Doors!

She clenches her fists it's happening again

One more smashed bottle the kids run to hide

They have a routine now it happens that often

They put there hands over there faces and watch
as there dad is terrified

This small dark space they hope is safe

In the closet holding each other shaking scared

She's been in their lives five years now

Calls herself their step mum it's clear she doesn't
care

This man's so kind hearted and caring

He's neither less or more than her size

Trying to protect himself hands defending

He begs her "Please Stop" with teary eyes

He's bleeding from his ears still it goes on

Now laid still on the cold kitchen floor

The girl covers her little brothers eyes

She knows her dad can't take anymore

The girls had enough hugs her brother Tells him stay in the closet hidden and safe

Her young heart pounds in her chest

She suppress the fear puts on her bravest face

She walks straight into the lions den

With as much strength as she can conger

One giant blow to the head

She manages to knock over the giant monster

The step mum now enraged

Stands back up puts the girl in her place

She's shouting and yelling

Blood now drips from this young girls face

The young girls gone quiet not one more scream

She kicks her and hits her till she can feel no more pain

Her poor dad unconscious and bleeding doesn't no things will never be the same

Her brother lets out an ear piercing scream!!

The woman looks down see's what she's done

Her heart starts to race

Panic takes over she slams the door and begins to run

The little boy sat on a bloody floor sobbing

The neighbours heard the screams they no somethings not right

Nobody knows the sight that awaits

The blue flashing lights were a little too late but awfully bright.

The Suicide Watch

(Dedicated to the police officers who deal with mental ill health with compassion)

You took a job hoping to save people's lives

You kiss your baby boy wave bye to your wife and start your shift

Never knowing what call you could attend

To try and make someone see like you that life's a gift

Racing through traffic, heart beat racing

You attend the scene compationate and strong

There's a vunerable person in front of you

You listen and try to understand what went wrong

Breakdowns don't discriminate

All sorts of people facing the end

People struggling feeling so low

You stand on the edge with them, try to help broken people mend

Men, Woman young and old

All sorts of issues they are dealing with

Mental health, grief and family breakdowns

A helpful supportive hand is always yours to give

Sadly though you can't always reason or pursuade

And sometimes they may fall

And I know it will stay with you but

Try to remember don't blame your self you didn't fail at all

You tried your best that's all that counts

Sometimes the demons are out of control and much to strong

You never stood a chance against what they were facing

Minds made up stood there to end it all along

But don't give up fingers crossed next time you'll win

So sincerely thankyou from all of us fallen and alive

Because you very rarely get credit

For not simply taking a less emotional nine to five.

Snakes and Ladders

You

You are not blind

But you do not see us

Down here

Amongst your disgarded crisp packets and the gum you spat out last week

Along with the bottle of water you just didnt have the time to bin

We arre

Whats the worb you used again?

Vermin?

Leaches on society?

The only thing were worthy of is to be dragged and laid on the railway tracks?!

Yet you call us vermin!

We are still sons and daughters

We are human just like you

Though you dont see us as so

We are not far apart

We have the same pieces the same moving parts

We could be only one pay check apart

Who knows when things could go wrong

I am simply down on my luck

Ive worked every dam day of my adult life

But i couldnt stop my factory from going bust

I got servence pay which covered the bills and the food

But i didnt have enough to pay the rent

Then no one gave a toss

I cried my first cold night underneath the starry sky

Now sat out here

All hope feels lost

I never really drank before except on htose special occasions

Now alchol eases my pain helps me feel less cold

I'd do anything for a leg back up

I've tried my self but no such look

So dont look upon me

With Discust and shameful eyes

Dont believe all the media's lies

Between money, alchol and food

I'd pick food every time!

Just look at me like i actuly exssit

Thats all i ask

Because been out here is bad enough without the memory of your Discust

As you walk past.

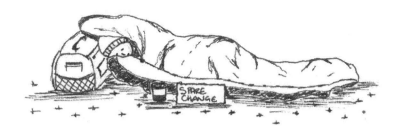

Stuck In An Aftershock

(Dedicated To Elaine)

There's a stranger in the hallway

She's fragile

Walks in stutters

Her body stuck in after shocks

Of an earthquake named Parkinsons

There's a stranger in the kitchen

Forgetting what she's doing

Trying to cook dinner in splashes and spills

Tremors taking there nasty hold

One vibration at a time

There's a stranger in the livingroom

Fast asleep in the middle of the day

Because restless legs have had her dancing

While she was suppose to be dreaming

There's even a stranger in the mirror

I see you

A ghost of who you were stares back

I can see the frustration and the torment in your eyes

Your stuck your stuck in a body

Thats been quaked into silence

Thats been quaked into dependence.

The Accountant

Do i count?

I don't mean mathamatically

Cause i've never been much good with numbers

I mean if i left the earth tomorrow

Would i have left a mark

Not a visble one of the tears and the sadness

But a mark

That would say

I definitly was here

I definitly lived

That i lived energetically

And reached for my dreams

And ignored all the fear

Do i count?

No not very well

But i can write

I can write poetry

Full of emotion and meaning

*Granted i can't f***ing spell*

But there's only me who's got to be reading

Do i count?

Yeah all the people i can share a connection with

The friends that i make smile

The friends that really get me

Do i count?

I count all the people i'm still trying to forgive

Including myself

Do i count?

I count all the days since my mental health spiralled out of control

Do i count?

I count all the people that have saved me so i'm still able to count.

Theres No Turning Back

Act One

Stood balancing on the edge

Between exsisting and just not

I don't stand here lightly

Looking fate in the face

Staring into the abyss

My chest is so tight

I can barely breath

Decisions, Decisions, Decisions

No Wait!

There's no decisions here

No choice!

No other clear avaliable road

Just fear and lonliness

Emptiness and Despair

Just my body balancing on this ledge

Act Two

Reason, pursuade and negotiate

That's what everyone else wants to do

Police tell me things will get better

They say my friends do care

Police want me to come back to safety

They want me safe and alive

In this moment···

They say they can get me help

They don't no this is the help i feel i need

They keep trying to talk me down

To keep me alive

They mention family

Friends

Tomorrow

That they don't want to see me die

They even say please

Act Three

Thoughts racing

Voices shouting

Over stimulation

Every bad comment i've ever heard

Playing on repeat in my head

I feel trapped

Suffocating in slience

Hearts pounding in my chest

I need to end the pain i feel

The suffering i've struggled

Through for years

I want everything just to freeze

I need everything just to stop

It's all just too much

I've been living for others for years

Tonight i do this for me

I step forward

Memories flash

The Ground 80ft away

Lights out

Curtain close

Act Four

All the pain left behind

The devastion

Mental ill health leaves in its shadows

So many unanswered questions

What if? Why?

Unrequited love

The girl that i never married

The kids I never had or got to meet

Anger, upset and confusion

Every person i've ever touched feels the hurt

Friends now just get the dial tone

No reply to messenger

Last online two years ago

Family photo's are now filled with broken hearts

Reminders are in my favourite songs and films

That loved one's will never see me again

That i'm no longer here

No more memories i'll make

Just an endless nothing

Just the end of my exsistance.

These Shoes weren't made for long distance running

Mom's cooking overwhelms my sences in happiness

Sisters laughing playing outside

Brother always crying and

Dad's making sphere's for the fishermen

The sun was setting as bad men tore through my peaceful village

Hot lights turned our homes into ashes

They turned mom and dad into bloody messes

Made me GASP for air on my own tears

They dragged me from safety from love from home

Made my brain fuzzy

I was forced to thinking killing was right

i was made to hurt so many people

My soul forever scared

I managed to escape

I ran, hid, starved, sweated and breath was hard at times

I coward, shook, i almost drowned i floated for

Hours and hours and more countless hours

Trembling to the bone with cold

I heard a ship in the distance

Speeding little boats came towards me

Foreign language out streatched arms and hands

Foreign soil saved me.

Gazes meet across classroom his beauty forbidden in the eyes of the law

Propaganda everywhere makes for uncomfortable skin

I see graffiti aimed at the me that is buried under the word normal/straight

I westle with pretend or truth

Heart racing

I see death threats and bloody men living there truth on the news

It's time pack a bag leave all i have built behind

Escape, run days pass by then months

A year goes by with what was left of my
innocence

Eventually privallaged soil

Eventually parades of pride

At last i am safe i am free.

Refugges aren't stats

Have some compassion

Have some empathy

They are people the same as you and i

But with scars and fears that made them flee

So stretch out your arms open your hands and

Make them a cup of good old english tea

Because were all running from something.

Warrior Women

This one is for all my female fighters

You struggle with health anxiety

Ive seen you struggle in its grasp

Ive seen you melt in its arms at the sight of blood

I try make you laugh through but i see how much it distress you

But

I saw you over come your fear

You had the op

I was proud

Though i never said the words out loud.

You fight with the f**ker of an illness M E

Its beaten you black and blue over the years

Its left its physical mark

It's hit you and knocked you sleepy laid on the ground

But you got your balance stood back on your feet

Just before the bell you were victorious and won that round.

You i've only seen you in person once on a holiday

But your in a god dam war for your life

There is no exhauration in that statement

But you look to god for guidence and light

You take up arms and wear your scar tarnished armor

Continue on Into the battlefield to fight

It takes a strong woman to walk into war

I pray someday you believe it.

You have been hurt you one of the nicest women i know

I don't know why he did that to you

I can't take away the hurt and the anger he caused

But i'm proud you didn't let the anger take control

It didn't eat you up inside

You didn't let this change the kind of person you are

Your small in physical size but your amazingly strong to keep your good heart

Cause good hearts tend to be changed by the world we live in all too often.

You i see you dragging around your heavy overflowing bag of hurts and scars

From the people who were supposed to love and respect you

Hurts from grief that you haven't been able to deal with yet

Hurts from your self

You were never taught that you were good enough

That you deserved love, kindness and respect

I see you learning that people care that not everyone is bad

Your learning that you count

That's what counts the most.

Your wrestling with addiction

With its nasty hold

You've seen discust and dissapointment in peoples eyes

Sometimes your tapping the mat screaming in submission

But

I've seen you grapple and hold it 1,2

But it breaks free

Before the referre gets to blow the whistle

Everytime you get pinned

You go away train and come back stronger

Eventually i know the referree will shout game over thats three.

You with the kids around your ankles

He ran away couldnt handle family life

But You can't run

Your achored to your responsabilities

Sometimes you cry your self to sleep at night

But you wake up in the morning and be a mum

You didn't give in when times were rough

You wiped away there tears and hugged them

You taught them skills to stay compassionate and tough.

I see you arguing with that voice in you head

It tells you the world would be a better place without you

It told you to fly without wings

But you hit the ground so hard it still hurts six years later

I see you shout and scream back that you deserve to be here

Though you don't actually believe it

I see you trying to help others in the things you do and say

I think others would agree

That's enough of a reason that you should stay

*To all my female fighters and i know theres more
than i mentioned*

You don't get enough recongnition

But i hope you could hear in this poem

That was my mission.

Young And Homeless

I sit and watch the hands of my broken watch

Tick Tock Tick Tock

Nothing to do

Nowhere to go

I see familar faces day by day

I'm invisable the people go by they don't see me
they don't no

They paint all homeless people with the same
brush

They assume it's my fault i'm sat cold and afraid
out here

That i must be a violent criminal

That i definitly have issues with drugs or beer

It doesn't cross their mind i had no choice

They don't understand i wasn't safe at home

Yeah that never crossed anyones mind

That's why now at night these streets i rome

With just my sleeping bag and a piece of cardboard

I don't wake up to a noisy alarm

I miss waking up indoors

I'm woken by the frosty chill running down my arm

I spend most days really stomach turning hungry

See i haven't got a kitchen to make some breakfast

I barely make enough change to buy a sandwhich

I've no cumfy bed to get a goodnights rest

I'm often moved on by police from doorway to doorway

See i am the HOMELESS YOUNG PERSON on the street

Some people spit on me and kick me

I have no warm place to call home or food to eat

I wish i was born to a family that cared

I'm the kid you don't see, even though you walk by me everyday

If you ever have a minute to talk to me

Take a second to hear·· "IT WASNT MY FAULT
I ENDED UP THIS WAY!"

Bloody Revenge!

If your reading this my body is lifeless and surrounded by crimson red

At last i'm at peace i'm finally dead

I needed so desperately to escape your suffocating grip

See no one believed me when i was alive

Because you have breasts they believed every one of your lies

They didn't beleive me at all, even with the bruises i had

I've been brought up well, i loved you couldn't bring myself to hit you

You got me so down the depression it just grew and grew

You'd come home scream and blame your bad day on me

I've made copies and sent them now i'll finally be free

Somehow you always managed to make me feel so small

Although this note i've left should at last see your downfall

You stopped me from seeing and going out with my friends

You've trapped me so much i'm facing the end.

Text message sent

You caught me sending a message for help!

You broke my phone not that you needed too!

See because i'm not brad pit and your beautiful

My friends are blind to the real abusive you

I needed to get out of this you'd taken all the confidence i had

Thank god you didn't discover this hidden writting pad

All i tried to do was love you

I don't no what happened to the girl i used too

You left me naked stripped me bare!

Society believes a woman cannot rape a man

I've left this note saying you did and they can.

Chapter 4

The Lighter Side Of Life

Yay you made it! now for the funny stuff, some of these poems i wrote as a sixty second challege for the spoken word night at cafe lux, or for Freedom For Girls Period Poverty charity nights theres also just some random stupid poems in there too just to make you smile so enjoy becasue i think im funny let's see what you think?

Oh How I Wish I Was Gravy!

Look at his smug little face sat over there

I've even seen his cousin advertised for something called KFC?

He looks and smells so good

Arrrgggghhhh Bisto!!

He gets the middle of the table it so isn't fair

With mash potatoes and puds they soak up the lot,

When i see the tinsel and the christmas tree

It gets worse he's in and out of the cuboard

I'm a bird's custard knock off

Because i'm from that Aldi store

I only cost 39p and still i feel under valued

Bet he comes from Waitrose where the prices are a rip off

I often catch myself wishing i was him

I've been here so long i swear soon i'll start to rust

I sit on this shelf collecting dust echooooo

I imagine if they drop him and start to grin

I try so hard to turn my yellow insides brown

But nothing!

No such luck!

My yellow face begins to frown

Why did i have to be a stupid tin of Aldi custard.

This is no laughing matter. Period.

I'm feeling pretty good

My first day off after two weeks

Of soild grueling shift work

Walking around the city centre

Window shopping and enjoying the sunshine

Then it happened

Like Siri had set some kind of an alarm

That i am unaware of

My insides awaken

After four weeks hibernation

They try to reach for freedom

The volcano erupts

The pain quakes and squeezes my abdomen

Cramps and spazms

Shoot through my stomach

Lava starts to flow

I'm afraid to say the only way it can

Towards the ground

Just like an electronic board at the doctors office

A thought flashes through my brain

Arrghh f**k... I'm wearing white

I looked fantastic as i left the house this morning!

I coordinated my outfit perfectly my trousers matched my hat.

Now it's like my trousers

Are the main chararter in a slasher movie!!

Panic stricken

My eyes clock the closet restroom

We've all done it ladies....

You no what i'm going to say

Piece after piece after god dam piece

Toilet rolled layed like the leaning tower of Piza

Folded and slotted in place

Which takes some Prosision i'll let you guys know!

Providing tempory security

For now!

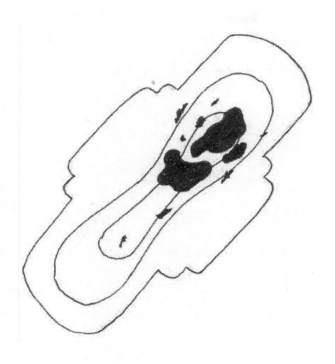

For The Love Of Socks

I absolutely love socks

I really do

Come on

Who doesn't love socks

Short socks, long socks

Warm socks, slipper socks

Stripped socks, spotty socks

Van socks

I just love all socks!

Some have holes well loved socks

Some have glitter and sparkles girl socks but definetly not my socks

Some have days of the week confused man socks

There's baby socks

Kid socks

And adult socks

Some people wear paired socks

Some wear odd socks which is totally weird and should never be done

There's grandad's christmas socks

Hideous socks

Birthday socks

Sock monkeys

Sock puppets

And lost socks

The washing machine loves any and all socks

However it only ever seems to eat one sock

Why does it never eat a pair

Maybe it doesn't like fruit

There's socks that shrink

There's socks that don't

For the love of all socks

Have i mentioned just how much i love socks!

Loop Swoop and Pull

Shoelace why do you have to tie me in knots

Since i was a kid you've always been so dam confusing

It's like down the rabbit hole, round the garden, put the f**king bins out

Why can't you be simple to tie your so frustrating.

I don't hate all laces let me just say im not a laciest

I happen to love the ones you can eat

I sit there quite happy chewing on the stawberry goodness

It's the only way i don't hit a lacey defeat.

You laces you always get stood on and then trip me up

I could use velcro but let's admit it isn't as cool

I just wish I could get you under control and make you stop laughing

I'm sick of you making me look like a god dam fool.

I get manda to tie all my laces for me

They last about four months until

They come lose and i end up flat on my f***ing face

That's it i'm going bare foot i've had my fill.

Argghh ok laces i'm sorry please forgive me

My feet are bloody freezing i want to wear my trainers now

I'm going to give you one last try

Nope there i am again tangled in you things holy f**king cow!!!

You god dam laces you know just what buttons to press to p**s me off

I'm really now at an absolute loss

*I love wearing my trainers they look cool with the
laces*

But by god have i realised laces are definitly

The boss!!

Lemon At The Checkout

Reconise me!!!

You god dam machine!!

Reconise me!!

God dam it!!

Im not just a lemon

Im a sour fruit

Im a dressing

Im a seasoning

I clean cookers make them sparkle

I'm polish

I'm shampoo

Im a f**king refreshing shower gel

I make the shit filled bathroom smell an ounce better once people flush

Im a lemon

I exsit

God dam it

Reconise me

I am lemon!

1,2 A Zombies Coming For You

Skin so pale and that stench of death

Don't get me started on thier rediculously bad breath

Thier limbs all broken, hanging off and thier shuffling walk

All they do it grr they can't hold a conversation or talk

Blood and guts dripping from there decaying jaws

They want the flesh you know is yours

There's no point in kicking and punching

Aim for the head or you'll be a zombie and it'll be flesh your munching

One hard blow to the head

Is the quickest way to put a zombie to bed

You better do it right

Because you won't recover from a bite

You have to be stealthy, you have to be quite

Sshhhh

Or you'll start a flesh eating riot

If your ever trapped by a herd

Cover your self in thier sent and don't move a muscle or say a word

If you see a zombie who's a loved one that's sadly turned

Don't get too close or you'll get burned

My best friend tried to save his dad

Guess what?

His dad was a zombie and for his lunch his sons organs he had

In a zombie apocolypse where no where is safe

You'll need al your wits about you to make an escape.

Period's You Suck!

Periods you suck!

I hate you cost me money

I hate you cost me tax on top of the money i already struggle to afford every month

When condoms can be found for free

Periods you suck!

I hate the cramps

I hate the heat

I hate having to check to see if ive leaked

Periods you suck!

I hate you in the summer

I try to avoid you on holidays

You make it scary to swim in the sea

I have visions that a sharks gunna jump up and eat me

Periods you suck!

Mother nature

I dont mind holding on to my lining this month

Come back later or maybe never

See you have the absolute worse f**king timing.

Coffee Table

I sit here

Day after day

I hold your handbags, your buiscuits

Sometimes even sticky jam sandwhices

I never get moved

Except maybe to hoover

And yet the language that comes out of your mouth

When you kick me

Like it's actually my fault

Is crazy

My feelings never get mentioned

No are you ok or sorry

Just OOCHH F**k, W**ker that F**king coffee table

Even though i've been here for the last 8 years

And i never move you know where i am

I'm right here!

You treat me so unfair

Then you expect me to hold your tea

And your bloody stinky feet

About which i never complain

All i ask is that you think of me

Say sorry when you kick me.

One last poem to leave you with...

Locked Down Surfer

I miss you

Its been way too long since i last saw you

Dont forget about me

I haven't dissapeared I haven't forgotten about you

Im been held by an ivisable enemy named covid

I swear im teeling the truth its not just some made up lie to simply try to avoid you

Nothing about this situation is simple

And i really miss you

God I miss you

The way you look so magestic when the sun bouces of your skin

The way you make the world feel so peaceful as you shimmer beneath the moonlight

The way you can make hours seem like minutes

The way you wave in barrels

Tumbling and roaring so strong and powerful

You take my breath away when i see you

Although i'm always aware you also have the power to take my breath away

I dream about you

The salty reside you leave on my face

The calm your able to enstill throughout my entire body

I practice my skills for you

I cant wait till the next time i get to ride you

The excitement i feel when i see you

Like a kid who's seeing the ocean for the very first time

Im ready now

Let me out

Let us all out

Im ready now!

Board in hand

Im ready to ride you until i cant ride anymore

Out of pure exhaustion and pain

I swear the next time i see you its going to be like the first time all over again

Until then···

I guess ill have to settle for

Youtube videos, Virtual Reality and my surfdoard
in my livingroom.

This is where i leave you, hope you enjoyed the ride...

The Dislexic Poet.

Baker Publishing

Printed in Poland
by Amazon Fulfillment
Poland Sp. z o.o., Wrocław

65795872R00069